20th
CENTURY ISSUES

MEDICAL ETHICS

Changing Attitudes 1900-2000

Robert Snedden

WAYLAND

TWENTIETH CENTURY ISSUES SERIES

Censorship
Crime and Punishment
Medical Ethics
Poverty
Racism
Women's Rights

Produced for Wayland Publishers Limited by Discovery Books Limited, Unit 3, 37 Watling Street, Leintwardine, Shropshire SY7 0LW, England

Editor: Patience Coster
Series editor: Alex Woolf
Series design: Mind's Eye Design, Lewes
Consultant: Dr Tom Wilkie

First published in 1999 by Wayland Publishers Limited, 61 Western Road, Hove, East Sussex BN3 1JD, England

NF.
170
SNE.

Acc: 11809 .

Find Wayland on the internet at http://www.wayland.co.uk

British Library Cataloguing in Publication Data
Snedden, Robert
  Medical ethics : changing attitudes 1900-2000. - (Twentieth century issues)
  1.Medical ethics - History - 20th century - Juvenile literature
  I.Title
  174.2

ISBN 0-7502-2215-8

Printed and bound in Italy by G. Canale & C.S.p.A., Turin

Picture acknowledgements
Corbis 24, 30 (Paul A Souders), 53, 55 (Richard T Nowitz); Corbis/Bettmann 9, 23, 34, 48, 50; Mary Evans Picture Library 10, 44; Mary Evans/Fawcett Library 19; Mary Evans/Sigmund Freud Copyrights/courtesy of W E Freud 45; Hulton Getty 6 (Richard Harrington), 25, 51; Impact 15 (Anita Corbin), 21 (Caroline Penn); Popperfoto 7, 8, 29, 31; Popperfoto/Reuter 41 (John C Hillery), 42 (Melbourne Age), 54 (Barbara Johnston), 57 (Jeff J Mitchell), 59; Press Association/Topham 37, 40; Topham Picturepoint 13, 16, 18 (Fiona Hanson), 26 (Paul Barker), 27, 47; Topham/Press Association 32; United Press Photos 49; Wayland Picture Library 4 (Tim Woodcock), 11, 14, 28; Wellcome Institute Library, London 5, 20, 22, 33, 39, 56.

Cover: main picture shows a mother with premature baby (Press Association/Topham); black-and-white pictures show, top to bottom, a travelling quack (Mary Evans Picture Library), administering penicillin during the Second World War (Wayland Picture Library); and a scientist examining a genetically-engineered mouse (Popperfoto/Reuter).

CONTENTS

ABOVE ALL, DO NO HARM

KEY MOMENT

The Hippocratic Oath

In Greece, at some point between the third and fifth centuries BC, physicians set out the first known series of guidelines for how doctors should think and behave. Over time these guidelines were attributed to one man, Hippocrates – the 'father of medicine' – and became known as the Hippocratic Oath. This counsels doctors to identify, or diagnose, illness from careful examination of the patient's condition. The Oath states that: 'I will follow that method of treatment, which, according to my ability and judgement, I consider for the benefit of my patients, and abstain from whatever is deleterious and mischievous....'

Ethics deals with the values of human life and with the sort of behaviour and actions that are approved of, or disapproved of, by society. It is about doing the right thing as we go about our daily activities. Medical ethics is a recent discipline, but its roots date back to the first time a person allowed him or herself to be treated by someone else. As soon as one person takes action that might affect the health and well-being of another, questions of ethics will inevitably arise. Medicine has always been concerned with ethics because it is about making choices between good and bad, right and wrong. A number of questions need to be answered before making these choices, for example: Will this form of treatment be good for the patient? Is it right to treat one person and not another?

Medical ethics is about the moral issues that surround medical decisions and the search for new forms of treatment and disease prevention. It involves the professions of medicine, nursing and the law, as well as philosophical considerations and religious beliefs. The term bioethics, which describes the study of ethical issues concerning living things, was introduced in the 1970s. Bioethics is concerned with the way in which we treat humans, and other animals, in the course of medical research. Bioethics also concerns the wider impact of medical science, beyond the practice of clinical medicine.

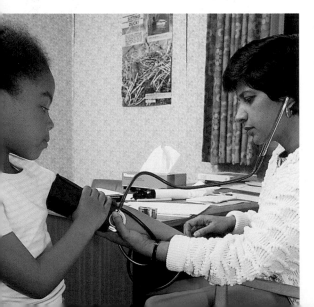

A doctor is constantly being called upon to take sometimes difficult decisions that will affect the health and well-being of a patient.

Long ago, Greek and Roman physicians and philosophers helped to establish medicine as a science. One of the most famous of these practitioners was Hippocrates, born around 460BC on the island of Cos off the south-west coast of Asia Minor. Hippocrates was a doctor, surgeon, scientist and artist who travelled throughout Greece for much of his life, teaching and practising medicine. He left many guidelines and instructions for doctors that remain valid to this day – the title of this chapter is just one of them.

The most famous set of guidelines to bear Hippocrates' name is the Hippocratic Oath. This states that a doctor's main aim is to help the patient and to treat all patients equally. Doctors are instructed not to pursue wealth or fame and to 'abstain from every voluntary act of mischief and corruption'. They are also instructed to regard personal information about their patients as private, never to be told to others. This 'Principle of Confidentiality' is still followed by doctors today.

LIBERTY AND DUTY

In eighteenth-century Britain, doctors and philosophers once again began to tackle the problems of medicine and ethics. Some of the guidelines formulated then would be considered unacceptable now. Thomas Percival published a code of ethics in which he openly suggested that the wishes of poor patients need not be treated as seriously as those of rich ones (understandable, perhaps, given that it was the rich patients that the doctor relied upon for his income!). Percival's guidelines were an attempt to avoid price-cutting competition between doctors. He was less concerned with the rights of patients. He did, however, maintain that: 'Every case… should be treated with attention, steadiness and humanity.'

Hippocrates (seated on the left) is sometimes known as the father of medicine. He founded a school of medicine on Cos that was the finest in the ancient world.

One of the foremost writers and thinkers on ethics was John Stuart Mill (1806-1873). In 1859 he published *On Liberty*, in which he set out his belief in the strong, perhaps absolute, right of people to determine the course of their own lives. In 1861 he published *Utilitarianism*, in which he advocated restricting the rights of the individual in the interests of the community in general. Although the two points of view may seem contradictory, Mill believed that they should work together. In other words, it is all right for people to live as they wish and believe what they like, but not at the cost of someone else's rights to the same freedoms.

Medical ethics embraces not only the techniques of modern medical science but also those of more ancient practices, such as acupuncture, especially as these become more popular as 'alternative' therapies in the Western world.

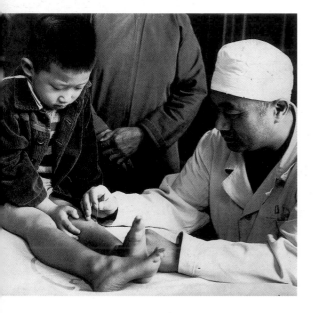

The notion of respect for the rights of the individual lies at the heart of medical ethics. For example, people sometimes refuse medical treatment for themselves or their children on the grounds of religious or other personal beliefs. One example of this is the refusal of Jehovah's Witnesses to allow blood transfusions. When these personal beliefs put the health of an individual at risk, questions arise as to the right of doctors to intervene. In situations such as this, it is the role of the medical ethicist to try and find a solution that respects both the individual and society.

DOCTORS AND DEATH CAMPS

In 1883 Francis Dalton coined the term eugenics (meaning well-born) to apply to the study and practice of breeding better plants and animals useful to humans, and also to the improvement of the human race. Eugenics found favour in the USA where it was considered to be at the forefront of scientific advance. It gave respectability to tough immigration laws that sought to keep entire ethnic groups from entering the USA. In 1927, the US Supreme Court upheld the performing of compulsory sterilizations, and some researchers advocated keeping people with low intelligence in colonies where they could be prevented from breeding.

Adolf Hitler, who was to become leader of the Nazi Party and later Fuhrer of Germany, praised American eugenics and convinced the German people that 'defectives' should be wiped out entirely. American researcher Jeremiah A Barondess, MD, has traced the involvement of German doctors in Nazi eugenics and uncovered the shocking fact that 'physicians joined the Nazi Party not only earlier, but in greater number than any other professional group'. We can only wonder at their reasons for doing so.

During the Second World War (1939-45), helpless human beings were subjected to inhuman experiments in the name of medical research. The Nazis, who ruled Germany from 1933-45 and subjugated much of Europe, treated whole races of people, in particular the Jews, as less than human. They inflicted unbelievable cruelties and degradations. According to Barondess, in addition to experimentation with Jewish prisoners in the concentration camps, Nazi doctors played a part in the killing of most of the one million victims of Auschwitz.

A similar situation could be found in the Far East, where the Japanese had the same attitude towards the people their armies conquered. How was it possible that a whole country had come to embrace ideals that treated other human beings as having no worth whatsoever? At the end of the Second World War, when Germany and Japan had been defeated, the atrocities that were uncovered shocked the world. Nazi and Japanese scientists and doctors had carried out the cruellest of experiments on prisoners. Shamefully, American authorities allowed the Japanese doctors to go free in exchange for the results of their research.

During the Second World War Nazi scientists and doctors carried out many painful and often fatal experiments on helpless prisoners. This unfortunate victim has been subjected to changes in air pressure.

OPINION

'Nazi medical ethics was an ethics of... racial purity, radical cleanliness and radical orderliness. Those subjected to medical experimentation were considered to be less than fully human in the Nazi scale of values.'
Dr Robert N Proctor, professor of the history of science, Pennsylvania State University, USA, 1996.

KEY MOMENT

The Geneva Declaration

The Geneva Declaration required doctors to take an oath, as follows: 'I solemnly pledge myself to consecrate my life to the service of humanity.... I will practise my profession with conscience and dignity; the health of my patient will be my first consideration; I will respect the secrets which are confided in me; I will maintain by all means in my power the honour and the noble traditions of the medical profession; my colleagues will be my brothers; I will not permit considerations of religion, nationality, race, party politics, or social standing to intervene between my duty and my patient; I will maintain the utmost respect for human life, from the time of conception; even under threat, I will not use my medical knowledge contrary to the laws of humanity....'

The trials at Nuremberg, where many Nazi doctors were brought to justice.

A NEW BEGINNING

Leading Nazis, including many doctors, were brought to trial at Nuremberg in 1946, accused of crimes against humanity. A set of ethical principles emerged from the Nuremberg trials. These principles became known as the Nuremberg Code. They were intended to ensure that medical research would never again be carried out in such a barbaric manner. The Code's first and most important point stated that: 'The voluntary consent of the subject is essential.' Point 9 of the code says that 'The human subject should be at liberty to bring the experiment to an end if he has reached the physical or mental state where continuation of the experiment seems to him to be impossible.' It is obvious that the Nazi doctors took their helpless victims far beyond this point.

The World Medical Association was founded in 1946. In 1948 it presented the Declaration of Geneva, which was intended to be a rewriting of the Hippocratic Oath in the light of the events that had taken place during the Second World War. The Geneva Declaration was in many ways an attempt to regain some notion of humanity from the horrors and inhumanities of the Nazi regime. It was an oath that was to be sworn not in the presence of God, but before the whole human race.

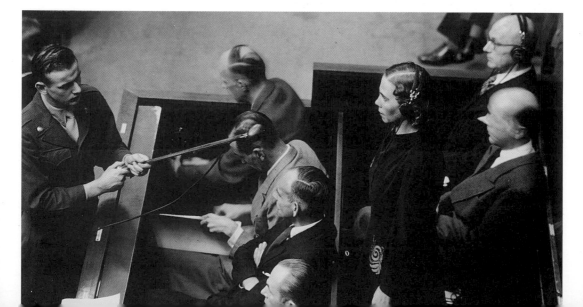

In 1949 the General Assembly of the newly-constituted United Nations adopted the International Code of Medical Ethics. This defined the duties of doctors in general – to the sick, and to each other. The Geneva Declaration formed part of this code.

In the 1960s and 1970s, medical ethics began to take on a new importance. Spurred on by the development of new techniques and knowledge, advances in medicine brought forth a range of ethical problems that had not even been dreamt of fifty years earlier. At the same time, social upheavals were taking place that encouraged people to demand new rights for themselves.

The signing of the Geneva Declaration in 1948 was a key moment in the history of medical ethics in which the medical establishment sought to distance itself from the inhumanities of the Nazi regime.

The field of bioethics came to prominence during the 1970s. In 1976, the Karen Ann Quinlan case involved the decision to remove a woman from a respirator after she had spent years in a coma. In its ruling on this case, the New Jersey Supreme Court suggested that bioethics consultations by in-house committees of doctors, social workers, attorneys and theologians should be considered as an alternative to legal action. In 1983, a US presidential commission urged hospitals to form ethics committees. Since 1992, all accredited hospitals in the USA must have either a bioethicist as a member of the staff or a procedure in place to handle ethics problems.

During the course of the twentieth century, science and technology have broadened the medical possibilities open to us. Also, social changes have affected our attitudes to science, technology and medicine. These, together with the revelation of abuses by doctors of patients subject to research, have brought about demands for others – ethicists and lawyers – to vet what used to be solely medical decisions.

OPINION

'Most doctors want to do good. But they're humans, and humans tend to be flawed.'
Arthur Caplan, bioethicist, University of Pennsylvania, USA, 1997.

MISTRUSTING THE MEDICS

In the past travelling salesmen would sell 'cures' that were of dubious value at best. Most of these 'medicines' were alcohol-based, and might make the patient feel better for a little while but wouldn't cure anything.

Until relatively recently there was no guarantee or certainty that the cures prescribed by doctors to their patients would have any beneficial effect at all. Before researchers uncovered the causes of disease and established what might best be used to treat them, prescribing medicine was very much a hit and miss affair – with a much higher likelihood of a miss than a hit. Patients would think nothing of dosing themselves with an elderly relative's patent cure-all, or buying a bottle of a miracle potion from a travelling salesman. If you got better, you got better. If not – well, that was just too bad. Ethics simply didn't enter into the picture.

The Industrial Revolution of the eighteenth and nineteenth centuries saw the migration of huge numbers of people to sprawling new towns and cities. These places were breeding grounds for all sorts of infectious diseases. Typhus, cholera, diphtheria and tuberculosis spread with appalling ease through the urban populations of Europe and North America. No one seemed to have any idea how these diseases could be treated. A breakthrough came in 1881 when the French physician Louis Pasteur unveiled the results of long experiments and his carefully constructed new germ theory of disease. He demonstrated that he had developed a safe and effective vaccine against anthrax. If invisible micro-organisms were the cause of disease, then surely it was only a matter of time before a way could be found of dealing with them all.

In 1910 the German chemist Paul Ehrlich introduced Salvarsan, a compound effective against the microscopic parasite that caused syphilis. The 1940s saw the arrival of penicillin, a seeming wonder-drug that was effective against a number of infectious diseases. Penicillin is an antibiotic, one of a group of chemicals obtained from moulds or bacteria that can be used to kill harmful bacteria. In the 1950s an effective treatment was at last found for tuberculosis with the discovery of streptomycin, another antibiotic. Around the same time, Jonas Salk developed a safe vaccine against polio. Vaccines stimulate the body's natural defences into attacking disease-causing viruses. People began to believe that medical science was on the brink of a new age in which disease would finally be conquered.

HUMAN GUINEA PIGS

After the Nuremberg trials of Nazi doctors, informed consent became central to human experimentation. Yet unethical experiments were still carried out in the USA, Britain and elsewhere. In the late 1940s, at Vanderbilt University in the USA, around 800 pregnant women were exposed to radiation to determine its effects on fetal development. Between 1946 and 1956, nineteen mentally retarded boys at the State Residential School in Fernald, Massachusetts, were fed radioactive iron and calcium in their breakfast cereal. Parents who consented to the study (supposedly to gather information about nutrition) were not told about the radioactive substances. Between 1963 and 1971, the testicles of 131 inmates at Oregon State and Washington State prisons were exposed to X-rays to find out what effect radiation might have on sperm production. The prisoners were not informed that cancer might result from exposure to radiation. These were not the only examples.

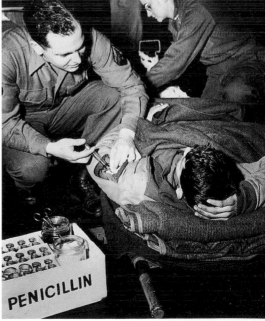

Penicillin, the first antibiotic to be discovered, saved countless lives in the Second World War and afterwards, helping to prevent death due to bacterial infections.

The price of miracles

In 1955 a safe vaccine to combat polio was successfully tested by Jonas Salk. In less than a month, over a million doses were administered in the USA with great success and public acclaim. According to the book *Patenting the Sun*, by Jane Smith, Salk, after first trying out the vaccine on himself and his laboratory staff, tested it on mentally retarded men and boys at a state institution in western Pennsylvania in 1952. The title of Smith's book is taken from a remark of Salk's. When Edward R. Murrow, a renowned TV commentator of the time, asked, 'Who will control the new pharmaceutical?' Salk replied that the discovery belonged to the public. 'There is no patent,' he said. 'Could you patent the sun?'

While working as a freelance medical tutor in Britain in the 1960s, Maurice Pappworth became increasingly concerned by descriptions of unethical experiments carried out on patients in hospitals in both Britain and the USA. He collected fourteen examples of ethically doubtful research, publishing them in 1962. His examples included experiments on children, the mentally defective and prison inmates. Pappworth created considerable outrage in the medical profession – most doctors were dismayed at their short-comings being held up to public display. However, Pappworth's actions helped to establish informed consent as a key principle of research, and ethics committees were consequently set up all over Britain to oversee projects.

In 1966, Professor Henry Beecher of the Harvard Medical School published an important paper in the *New England Journal of Medicine* detailing a variety of abuses of human subjects in medical research at major universities and medical centres in the USA. He claimed to have found twenty-two obvious abuses of human subjects in the recent medical literature. These included research carried out on subjects who had not been offered the option of standard treatment, and the use of subjects without their consent. Beecher's article triggered a series of debates inside and outside the medical profession on the importance of obtaining consent from research subjects or someone who could speak on their behalf.

One of the most infamous abuses of medical research was the Tuskegee syphilis study, which looked at the course of the disease and its long-term degenerative effects on the nervous system. From the early 1930s to the early 1970s, public health service doctors in the USA studied more than 400 black men with syphilis in Macon County, Alabama. The men were not told that they had the disease, nor were they ever offered treatment. When the story emerged, people were horrified to learn that the first point of the

Nuremberg Code, the 'voluntary consent of the human subject', had been abused in America. The US government appointed a commission to investigate the scandal and recommendations based on its findings were incorporated into health services regulations in 1981. As a result of the Tuskegee scandal, the requirement for voluntary consent in research became law in the USA.

VACCINES

Some of the greatest medical achievements of the twentieth century have involved finding vaccines against childhood diseases. But this raises the difficult issue of whether research should be conducted on children. During the development of these vaccines researchers have had no alternative but to do so – there is no other way to test how effective a vaccine might be. The problem is that children, particularly the very young, are not capable of granting informed consent. The only solution is to obtain the consent of the parent or guardian of the child.

In 1997 there was outrage in Australia when it was revealed that hundreds of orphan babies and small children had been used as 'guinea pigs' in experiments on vaccines. These tests – of cures for herpes, whooping cough, influenza and other diseases – had been carried out over twenty-five years, from 1945 to 1970. Some of the experiments had failed to pass safety tests in animals and had caused vomiting, abscesses and other side effects in the children. No attempt had been made to obtain consent from the relatives or guardians of the children involved.

Jonas Salk, developer of a safe vaccine against polio, inoculates a boy during mass trials of the vaccine in Pittsburgh in 1957.

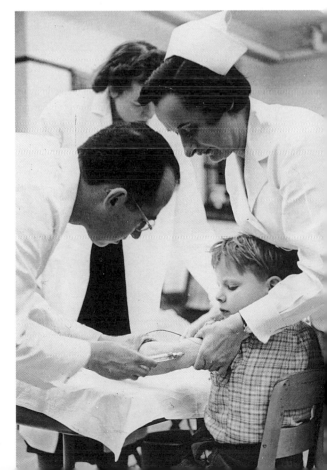

OPINION

'Informed consent should not be considered a document to protect funding agencies, institutions or the investigator from legal liability. The reason for informed consent is to protect the volunteer.'
Dr Roberto Rivera, corporate director of international medical affairs at Family Health International, USA, 1994.

In the 1950s and 60s, thousands of children were born with limb and other defects as a result of their mothers having been prescribed thalidomide during pregnancy.

RESISTANCE MOVEMENTS

In the 1960s, people began to cast doubt on the achievements of medical science. They argued that the battle against disease was being won by improved hygiene and better diet, as standards of living improved. Antibiotics were simply helping an already improved situation. Some people began to suggest that medicine, far from being a force for good, was actually harmful. Ivan Illich, a sociologist and former priest, became a particular scourge of the medical establishment, as he spoke of iatrogenic, or doctor-caused, illness. His best known book on the subject, *Medical Nemesis*, was first published in 1975 and reissued in 1995 as *Limits to Medicine*. One example Illich cited of doctor-caused illness was the tragic case of thalidomide.

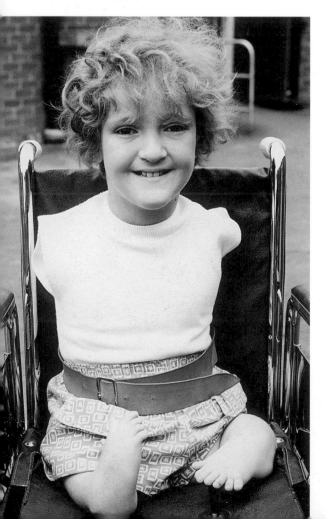

The drug thalidomide was introduced in 1958 as a sedative and a safe cure for women suffering from morning sickness during pregnancy. The 'safe cure' soon became a nightmare as, over the next three years, thousands of children were born with malformed limbs and internal defects. An estimated 12,000 babies worldwide were born damaged as a result of their mothers having been prescribed thalidomide. Half of the children died in infancy. The USA was spared the thalidomide disaster because the Food and Drug Administration (FDA) did not approve the drug for general use, largely because of unanswered questions about its side effects. In 1962, the US Congress, recognizing the worth of caution, granted the FDA greatly expanded powers to regulate drugs.

One consequence of the thalidomide tragedy was that women of reproductive age were excluded from many drug trials. However, because women and men react differently to medications, women have since sought the right to be involved equally in research to ensure that drugs are developed that will meet their needs.

WHAT'S THE ALTERNATIVE?

Undoubtedly medical science is helping people to live longer – but at what cost? As people grow older they become ever more dependent on the health-care establishment and the costs of looking after them are ever increasing. And perhaps the attempts to increase the length of life too often ignore what the quality of that life might be.

At the end of the twentieth century people have come to be suspicious of the 'big brother' medical establishment. In the last three decades, people have eagerly adopted so-called 'alternative' therapies, such as homeopathy, reflexology and faith healing. Two out of five doctors in Britain will refer patients to alternative therapists. The one-to-one nature of alternative health practice is no doubt part of its appeal. In contrast with conventional medicine, which treats the diseased organ, many alternative therapies claim to treat the whole person. Perhaps alternative medicine helps people to feel more in control of what is happening to them, more cared for, in spite of the fact that the 'care' may come with a large price tag attached. Undoubtedly, some practitioners of New Age therapies can be quite as manipulative and as ready to take advantage of the trust of their clients as any high-tech member of the medical profession.

Homeopathy uses solutions of plant and other substances that are so highly diluted that practically no trace of the active ingredient remains. Studies have shown that homeopathic remedies can have a positive effect, but many scientists believe that the effect is psychological rather than physical.

> ### KEY MOMENT
> #### From Nuremberg to Helsinki
> In 1946, the judges at the Nuremberg trial set out ten principles, the first of which is that 'the voluntary consent of the human subject is absolutely essential.' This primary principle was slightly watered down by the Declaration of Helsinki in 1964, a statement of research ethics drawn up not by judges but by the doctors of the World Medical Association. Helsinki permits research without consent if the doctor considers it essential not to obtain informed consent. The reasons for doing so have to be set out before an independent committee. In 1996, the US Food and Drug Administration issued a directive permitting experimental procedures to be carried out without their consent on patients facing life-threatening medical conditions.

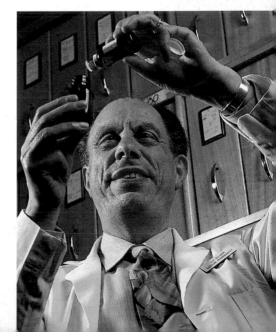

REPRODUCTIVE RIGHTS

Some of the greatest dilemmas the bioethicist has to face have resulted from advances in the medicine of reproduction. Most of these issues concern the rights of humans to control their bodies. In the case of women, throughout the century there has been great debate about their rights over the embryo that can develop from the sex cells they carry in their bodies.

Some women prefer not to be surrounded by medics when they give birth – a choice not available to most of the world's women who have little access to medical care.

Children, and mothers, are much more likely to survive the traumas of birth now than they were in Victorian times. In some Victorian maternity hospitals as many as one in ten women might die in childbirth. For those who didn't make it to hospital, giving birth at home was also risky. It was only in 1902 that midwives had to be registered; before then women with the scantiest training or knowledge might assist at the birth of a child. Today in the West the risks of death in childbirth are less than one in 10,000. However, we see more and more women opting to have their children at home rather than in the virtual safety of the maternity unit. This may be a reaction against antiseptic hospital conditions, and the sometimes undesired intervention of highly-trained medics – but is it a rational choice?

In 1942, a physician called Grantly Dick-Read published a book entitled *Childbirth Without Fear*. It became a bestseller. In it he argued that women had become frightened of childbirth, in part because doctors had made them afraid by interfering in what was, after all, a natural process. In 1956, the National Childbirth Trust was set up to promote his ideas. Dick-Read's natural methods were at odds with the medical establishment's preference for production-line child deliveries, in which a woman who didn't go into labour at the desired time could be injected with a drug to help her do so.

By the 1980s, maternity units had become seemingly much more enlightened places. Women were allowed to choose the position in which they wanted to give birth and the pain relief they would have. They could also specify the people they wanted to be present to assist them at the birth. Nevertheless, even now there is still the background presence of a team of medics ready to rush in and take over should the birth not go according to plan.

SAVE THE CHILDREN?

Every day, in hospitals around the world, children are born who would have no hope of survival without medical intervention. Just a few decades ago the question of what to do with a severely handicapped new-born would not have arisen. The skills and technology did not exist to make saving it a possibility. Before doctors and scientists learned the skills and techniques necessary to keep them alive, babies born prematurely under about a kilogram in weight were unlikely to survive. By the 1980s at least half could be kept alive, and the odds are improving all the time.

The cost of this care is colossal, and not just in financial terms. In 1990 the cost of maintaining new-born intensive care units in the USA was calculated to be $2.6 billion a year. The unfortunate fact is that, despite all this care, half of the children who survive face a lifetime of disability and suffering. In the USA doctors are required by law to treat all babies except those for whom treatment would produce no benefit.

Advances in childcare mean that premature babies who would once have been doomed now have a chance of survival.

In a recent controversial case, a baby born with no higher brain, and therefore no hope of anything approaching a normal life, was kept alive on a ventilator at the insistence of the mother. She believed that any human life, even one as severely limited as this, was worth saving no matter what the cost. Doctors urged that the ventilator be switched off, but the mother refused. The child died in April 1995. Meeting the mother's wishes was undoubtedly expensive. The ethical problem that arises is the issue of resource scarcity versus respect for all human life, whatever form it takes.

In Britain, the prospects of the new-born are monitored and re-evaluated. If severe brain damage or death seems likely, efforts to keep the child alive are stopped after the medical team have consulted with the child's parents. In Sweden, no efforts are made to treat babies that have little chance of survival. In France, the doctors' judgement overrides that of the parents in the case of a severely brain-damaged child. For many people, who believe that life has a value regardless of whether a person is handicapped or not, this attitude is indefensible. But how, with limited funds and expertise, can all cases be treated equally? Choices have to be made. Should health-care organizations have rationing policies? Should we set limits on the amount of time and money we, as a society, are prepared to spend on individual cases? There are no easy answers to these questions and probably never will be.

THE RIGHT TO CHOOSE

In the early 1910s, Margaret Sanger (1879-1966) worked as a maternity nurse on the Lower East Side of New York, delivering the babies of poor, mostly immigrant women who suffered the pain of frequent childbirth, miscarriage and abortion. The women she attended knew nothing of how to prevent pregnancy. The 1873 Comstock Law, in force in the USA at the time, upheld 'decency' in society and prohibited discussion of birth control, even between a doctor and his patient. Public libraries were forbidden to hold books on contraception. Many women turned to illegal back-street abortionists, risking injury and death.

Sanger began to mount a challenge to the Comstock Law. In 1912 she started a column on sex education for the *New York Call* entitled 'What Every Girl Should Know'. In 1914 she published the first issue of *The Woman Rebel*, advocating the use of contraception. In 1916, Sanger was arrested and imprisoned for opening a birth control clinic in Brooklyn, New York. When she appealed against her conviction, the New York State appellate court issued a ruling that exempted doctors from the law prohibiting providing contraceptive information to women if it was prescribed for medical reasons. This loophole allowed Sanger to open a legal doctor-run birth control clinic in 1923. Finally, in 1936, American doctors were given the right to prescribe and distribute contraceptives.

Despite her achievements as a pioneer of the birth control movement, Margaret Sanger's reputation was tainted by her association with the eugenics movement. She gave support to the idea of sterilizing the mentally incompetent, and saw birth control as a means of preventing the spread of mental and physical defects.

*At ten to twelve weeks a fetus is
recognizably human although it
would not be able to survive outside
the womb. Ideas as to when the
fetus becomes a person range from
conception to birth. Denying
'personhood' to the fetus makes
termination easier to contemplate.
For those who believe that
humanity begins at conception the
idea of termination is repugnant
and equivalent to murder.*

PRO-LIFE OR PRO-CHOICE?

In 1967, the British government passed the Abortion
Act, making abortion legal. Britain was the first country
in the world to do so. Many of the doctors and other
people who were involved in campaigning for the Act
were motivated by the thousands of cases every year of
women whose back-street or self-induced abortions
went terribly wrong. Many died as a result. Since the
Abortion Act was passed, pro-life campaigners have
sought to have it overturned. Anti-abortion campaigner
Jack Scarisbrick says, 'We have to keep coming back to
the fundamentals. What happens when an abortion is
done? A human being is killed.'

The argument concerning when it is that an embryo
becomes human lies at the very heart of the abortion
debate. The Roman Catholic Church, which is
steadfastly opposed to abortion, is committed to the view
that the fetus becomes a person at some time before
birth. However, it will not say exactly when this happens.
In 1973 the Roe v Wade ruling in the USA concluded
that it was reasonable to assume that the fetus was not a
person and did not have the rights of a person.

Another factor to be taken into account is the
increasing ability of doctors to keep premature infants
alive. In Britain, the 1967 Abortion Act set a limit of
twenty-eight weeks after conception for abortion, and
in the USA the 1973 Supreme Court ruling set a
limit of six months. These limits were set partly on
the grounds that a fetus could
not survive outside the womb
before then. This is obviously
no longer the case. In 1990 the
British government passed the
Human Fertilization and
Embryology Act. While this
reduced the time limit for
abortion from twenty-eight to
twenty-four weeks it also

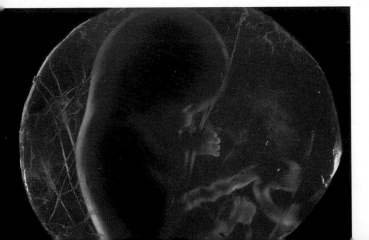

introduced a provision for abortion to be carried out right up to full term in exceptional circumstances. It also permitted selective reduction of embryos in a multiple pregnancy.

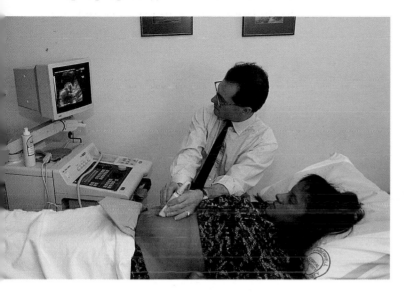

Ultrasound scans can be used to pick up some fetal defects or to determine sex. A woman might decide to terminate the pregnancy as a result of the scan.

The ability to carry out selective reduction in the case of a multiple pregnancy is a further complication to the abortion debate. This procedure is performed before the third month of pregnancy by injecting selected fetuses with potassium chloride, which stops the heart. For some, the moral dilemma that this presents is profound. Multiple pregnancies are one of the commonest risks faced by people undergoing treatment with fertility drugs. People previously unable to conceive are sometimes faced with the tragic irony of having to destroy fetuses to ensure the survival of those that remain. Fetuses in a multiple pregnancy are far more susceptible to miscarriage, premature birth, birth defects and low birth weight. Other people may want to use the selective reduction technique for practical, rather than medical, reasons. Benjamin Younger, executive director of the American Society for Reproductive Medicine, said, 'There are patients that will push very hard to reduce from three fetuses to two. They'll say, "Doctor, I can't cope with triplets." '

OPINION

'Just because something is legal doesn't mean it's right. The Supreme Court decision in Roe v Wade was made with the implicit view that abortion would be a desperate personal choice in circumstances in which there was no better option.' Lisa Sowle Cahill, member of the National Advisory Board on Ethics and Reproduction, 1998.

KEY MOMENT

The Pill

In 1950, American biologist Gregory Pincus was invited by Margaret Sanger's Planned Parenthood Federation to develop an ideal contraceptive. By 1955 an oral birth control pill was being tested on 6,000 women from Puerto Rico and Haiti. In 1960, the first oral contraceptive, called Enovid-10, was launched in the USA. The 'Pill', as it became known, brought about a revolution in birth control. Despite its popularity there were worries about health risks. As early as 1961 studies showed that the high levels of hormones in the Pill carried the risk of blood clots, heart attacks and strokes. In 1962 there was evidence of at least eleven Pill-related deaths.

In the 1980s French researchers developed RU-486, a drug that can induce abortion without the need for invasive surgical procedures. RU-486, also known as Mifepristone, works during early pregnancy disrupting production of the hormone progesterone. When progesterone production stops, the lining of the uterus is shed, and the embryo along with it. In tests carried out in the USA, RU-486 ended pregnancies in ninety-two per cent of women. The FDA has determined that RU-486 is safe and effective, but the House of Representatives voted to block federal approval of RU-486 and similar abortion-inducing drugs. The drug's US developer hoped to put RU-486 on the market in 1999. The drug is widely available in Europe. In Britain, for example, it is approved for use up to sixty-three days after conception.

CONTRACEPTION

The right, or at least the ability, to choose whether or not to have a child reaches back beyond the point of conception. More or less haphazard means of contraception have probably been around since the time when people first learned how babies are made. In the 1920s and 1930s, investigations began into the working of human sex hormones. These are biochemicals that regulate the functions of the body's

The contraceptive pill has helped to free countless women from the fear of an unwanted pregnancy. However, there can be undesirable side effects and its use is forbidden by the Catholic Church, which sees it as interfering with the natural process of procreation.

organs according to its requirements. In 1951 in the United States, Luis Miramontes synthesized a biologically more active modification of the female hormone progesterone. Experiments soon showed that this substance would inhibit ovulation. The researchers were not interested in using this as a method of birth control. However, Margaret Sanger became involved and arranged for a large grant to be made to carry out research into hormonal birth control.

The abortion debate divides into pro-choice, which advocates the woman's right to determine the fate of the fetus she carries, and pro-life, which defends the notion of the fetus as a human in its own right.

In 1955, trials of the new birth control method were carried out amongst poor women in Puerto Rico. The ethical problems of conducting experiments on people in this way should be obvious. In 1959, the FDA approved the first oral contraceptive. The introduction of birth-control pills in 1960 was so successful that within a year a million women in the USA were using them.

In the late 1960s the burgeoning women's movement viewed birth control as part of a woman's rights to self-determination, not just as a means of family planning. The ready availability of the 'Pill' freed a generation of women from the fear of pregnancy. Scant regard was paid to the dosage being administered, however, and side effects such as thrombosis and jaundice soon became apparent. The exposure of these health dangers helped to spark a powerful women's health movement. Today the amounts of hormone contained within contraceptive pills are strictly controlled. However, many women reject this method of birth control, seeing it as an undesirable interference with their natural body chemistry.

KEY MOMENT

The Dalkon Shield

Intrauterine devices (IUD) were mass-marketed from the late 1960s as a reliable form of contraception. The Dalkon Shield IUD caused at least twenty deaths and hundreds of thousands of severe infections and injuries, often resulting in permanent sterility. The manufacturer, A H Robins was successfully taken to court by many of the victims and shown to have ignored warnings of the dangers from its own staff. Nearly all forms of IUD, including those with good safety records, were removed from the US market as a result.

EMBRYO ETHICS

A further ethical problem concerns the obtaining and use of human embryos. As every embryo has at least the potential to become a fully-fledged human being, what are its rights? In 1982 the British Medical Research Council ruled that, provided both donors agreed, experiments on human embryos were acceptable for approved research purposes. There must be no attempt to culture the embryo beyond the stage when implantation became possible or indeed any intention to implant it in the uterus. In 1984 a commission chaired by Mary Warnock issued a report in which it proposed to limit any experimentation to within fourteen days from fertilization. In 1990 the British Parliament voted to continue to allow experiments on embryos up to fourteen days old, under the control of the Human Fertilization and Embryology Authority.

During in vitro fertilization an egg is fertilized outside the body and then implanted in the mother's womb. Before it was shown to be safe many thought it unethical to risk a procedure that might result in a deformed child.

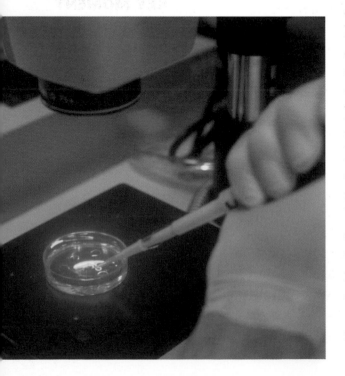

The birth of the first 'test-tube baby', Louise Brown, took place in Britain in 1978. Since then a variety of *in vitro* fertilization (IVF) techniques have been developed. What once made headlines has now become commonplace. In 1994 alone, 6,000 test-tube babies were born in the USA. In that year, the US National Institutes of Health set up an ethics panel specifically to look into the question of human embryo research. The group recommended that, in certain limited instances, government scientists should be permitted to use 'spare embryos' obtained from fertility clinics or to create human embryos for research. There was an instant outcry and within twenty-four hours President Clinton had intervened to declare that the government would not fund scientists who created embryos for research. Congress later effectively banned all embryo studies.

The Warnock Report also condemned surrogacy. This is when one woman agrees to undergo a pregnancy for another woman. The baby may be conceived from the surrogate mother's egg and the contractual father's sperm, or a couple can have an embryo conceived using their own sperm and egg implanted into the surrogate mother's uterus. Surrogacy gives a woman for whom pregnancy is impossible or health-threatening the chance to have a child that is biologically hers. It is also possible for a person to 'have' a baby by obtaining eggs and sperm from donors and hiring a surrogate to go through with the pregnancy. It is even possible for a woman to use a surrogate for cosmetic reasons or convenience alone.

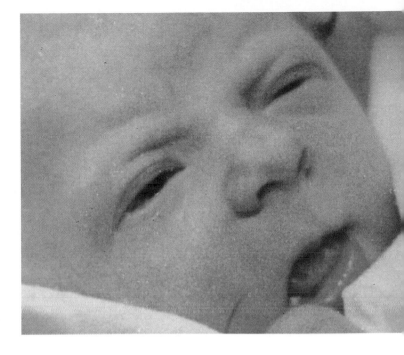

Before Louise Brown (above) was born in 1978 no human had ever started life outside the body of its mother. She was the proof that IVF could be performed safely. It is now a common procedure.

Such commercial surrogacy is practised in some European countries and in the USA. In the UK, under the Surrogacy Arrangements Act 1985, it became illegal for anyone to pay someone else to have a child on their behalf. The Act did not affect non-commercial surrogacy agencies. Under the Human Fertilization and Embryo Act (HFEA) of 1990, a statutory licensing authority was established to regulate research and treatment in human infertility and embryology. The act brought surrogacy services within the control of the Human Fertilization and Embryology Authority.

OPINION

'When you take reproduction out of its natural context it's bound to throw up problems. Of course it's a slippery concept – what's natural, what's normal – but it is a notion which still has some use.'
Pat Walsh of the Centre for Medical Law and Ethics at King's College, London, on surrogacy, 1997.

OPINION

'In the United States, our policies develop from the individual cases up. The European system tries to design the dog and let it wag its tail. We have fifty or a hundred or 150 wagging tails from which we then try to reconstruct the dog.'
R. Alta Charo, a medical ethicist at the University of Wisconsin and member of the president's bioethics panel, on the problems of drawing up surrogacy legislation.

The health-care system in the USA is quite different from that in Britain. American health-care is private, which in part explains why there has been no legislation along the lines of the Surrogacy Arrangements Act or the HFEA. It is often a matter of doctors and their patients deciding for themselves what is best, rather than having the law decide for them. Only when there is a dispute do cases come to court for a decision. Even then the result will depend on the prejudices of the judge involved.

TOO OLD TO BE A MOTHER?

In 1990, doctors established the technique of implanting women past normal childbearing age with embryos formed from donated eggs. Since then, more than a hundred such pregnancies have been carried through. The women concerned have to be treated with the hormones oestrogen and progesterone to enable the pregnancy to proceed to term.

A technician prepares to freeze embryos at an IVF clinic. It is now possible for a man and woman to have embryos kept frozen until such time as they wish to have children. This has sometimes resulted in legal battles for custody of the embryos when the couple later separate.

In 1997, a sixty-three-year-old Californian woman gave birth to a baby girl. The woman had never been pregnant before. The medical team who treated her believed that she was fifty years old when she first came to them. Nothing in her medical records or arising from the treatment indicated that she was lying. After a few years, the medics succeeded in implanting a thawed frozen embryo in the woman's uterus and establishing a pregnancy.

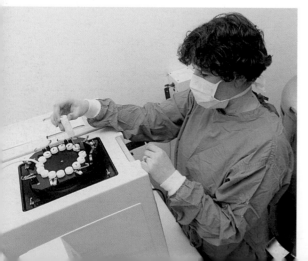

These cases raise a number of ethical issues. First, perhaps, is the question of at what age it becomes 'unnatural' for a woman to have a child. It is not unusual to read newspaper articles that tell of men fathering children in their seventies or eighties. Generally the men are referred to in glowing terms: their ability to become fathers at such a great age is seen as a demonstration of their virility. However, when a woman in her sixties has a baby, the reaction may be one of outrage accompanied by demands that these 'unnatural practices' be stopped.

The purpose of medicine is another issue raised by these examples. Does medicine exist to maintain and restore normal function to the human body, keeping it healthy and putting things right when they go wrong? Or should it expand the capabilities of the body, extending and pushing the boundaries of what we understand 'normal' to be? Menopause is, after all, a natural condition, so should we be spending time and resources trying to undo its consequences?

What about the rights of the child? People have argued that an older mother might not have the reserves of energy necessary to cope with bringing up an active young child. But on those grounds it could be argued that a woman with a physical handicap should be barred from having children, or that mothers who go out to work should not have children either.

Techniques are being developed that would allow a child to be born to a mother who was never born herself. The answer to this seeming riddle lies in research carried out in the early 1990s, when a method was devised of taking eggs from the ovaries of aborted female fetuses. The eggs were fertilized and implanted in the wombs of mature females, who proceeded in due course to give birth. So far the procedure has only been carried out on mice but it can only be a matter of time before it is carried out on a human. The ethical issues that this will raise are profound indeed.

This photograph illustrates some of the complex issues that can arise from surrogacy. In this case the surrogate mother (shown here with her husband) gave birth to twins, a boy and a girl. The boy, shown in the picture, was rejected by the contractual father who only wanted a girl.

THE BODY SHOP

There are many occasions on which a doctor cannot treat a condition simply by prescribing drugs. Sometimes it is necessary to carry out physical repairs. Surgery is the branch of medicine concerned with the treatment of injuries and illnesses, by means of an operation.

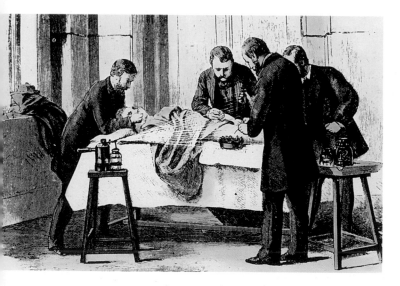

The introduction of anaesthetics and antiseptics into the operating theatre dramatically reduced the number of deaths following surgery.

The nineteenth century saw the two greatest advances to occur in surgical practice. For centuries surgery had been an excruciatingly painful process that was likely to end in the patient's death, either from shock or infection. The development of safe and reliable methods of anaesthesia, especially the discovery of ether in the 1840s, was a great step forward. Coupled with the introduction of antiseptic methods in operating theatres, pioneered by Joseph Lister in the 1860s, the way was open for surgeons to begin to contemplate carrying out lengthy and difficult operations that would have been impossible before.

The beginning of the twentieth century saw surgeons gaining rapidly in confidence, equipped with new tools such as x-rays (discovered by Karl Röntgen in 1895), which allowed them to see into the body before a single cut was made. Some surgeons appeared to be over-enthusiastic in their willingness to operate. 'Hitching up the kidneys' was recommended as a cure for back pain, for example. Because most people had such an unwavering respect for doctors at the time, and because of the lack of information available to the patient, such questionable 'treatments' went virtually unchallenged.

Surgery was transformed from simply cutting out damaged parts and hoping for the best into a sophisticated repair and (as the century progressed) replacement process. As early as 1869 Felix Guyon, in Paris, discovered that small pieces of skin could be transplanted from one part of the body to another to help the healing of wounds. Skin transplants came to the fore in the First World War when surgeons had to treat horrific injuries. Harold Gillies, one of the leading plastic surgeons of the time, dealt with 2,000 cases of facial damage after the Battle of the Somme in 1916. Gillies' assistant, Archibald McIndoe, went on to treat injured airmen in the Second World War – his skills in reconstructive surgery giving badly disfigured people the chance of a normal life.

Plastic surgery or cosmetic surgery, as it became known, was soon being used to treat people who were simply dissatisfied with their appearance and could afford to have it altered. The plastic surgeon could straighten noses and tighten sagging skin. Breast implants, originally developed for women who had lost their breasts as a result of cancer, were inserted into healthy women who wanted to change their looks. Ethically the argument is between condemning these procedures as an unnecessary use of scarce medical resources (a crooked nose isn't life threatening) and seeing them as addressing a psychological need in the 'sufferer'.

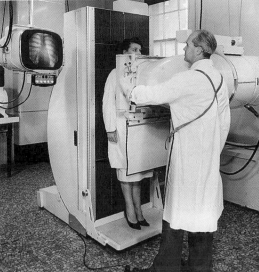

Performing an x-ray at Guy's Hospital, London, in 1961.

KEY MOMENT

The dangers of x-rays

X-rays were first used for clinical purposes in 1896, and experiments were soon being carried out around the world. The damaging effects of x-rays were soon recognized. Because there was no sensation and no immediate reaction to x-ray exposure, many experimenters accidentally overexposed their hands. It soon became apparent that x-rays could produce a reaction similar to sunburn, except that the damage to the skin was deeper and more permanent. The resulting ulcers frequently became cancerous and many of the early workers with x-rays had to have fingers or hands amputated. In some cases they died.

THE DONATION DILEMMA

In 1900 Karl Landsteiner took the first steps towards establishing the existence of different blood groups; this opened the way for safe blood transfusions. At the end of the 1930s, blood banks were established for the first time in anticipation of severe casualties resulting from the Second World War. By the 1950s, blood transfusions were an everyday part of medical care. In the private health-care system of the USA, blood banks come in two varieties: commercial suppliers, which pay blood donors; and non-profit collection centres, which depend on voluntary donations. Most transfusions are carried out using donated blood, while the commercial banks supply almost all of the blood used by the pharmaceutical industry to develop vaccines and drugs.

A man prepares to donate blood. In many countries people can make substantial amounts of money from selling their blood. Others would consider it morally reprehensible to ask for money in return for donated blood.

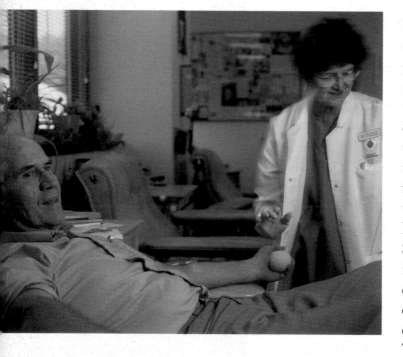

Paid blood donors can earn from $50 to $500 per pint, depending on the rarity of their blood type. As most healthy donors can safely part with two pints a week, this makes a tempting financial incentive for the less well off. The League of Red Cross Societies and other international organizations are concerned about the exploitation of donors. The difficulty they face is that blood is not seen in the same light as, say, a kidney. Our bodies can always make more blood. The United States National Organ Transplant Act (NOTA), banned the sale of organs for transplant in 1984, but excluded 'replenishable tissues such as blood or sperm' from the ban.

Kidneys were one of the first organs to be transplanted in humans. Kidney transplantation in animals was first performed in 1902, but serious attempts at human kidney transplantation were not begun until about 1950 in Boston, Massachusetts. In these early transplantations the kidneys were implanted in the thigh because this was easier to achieve, but techniques were later developed to position the kidney more normally.

In 1967 the South African surgeon Christiaan Barnard sewed a dead woman's heart into his patient Louis Washkansky. The patient died eighteen days later but Barnard's operation was hailed throughout the world. The following year a committee at Harvard Medical School recommended that the definition of death be changed from when the heart stopped beating to when the brain ceased to function. This would allow the 'harvesting' of hearts from people who were brain dead but whose breathing was sustained by means of an artificial respirator. Today the concept of brain death has won widespread acceptance.

In 1959 the discovery of drugs that interfered with the body's natural tendency to reject foreign objects made transplantation much more successful. The downside is that transplant patients must take these drugs for the rest of their lives. If they take too little, the organ will be rejected; if they take too much, they will not be able to fight off infections. Organ transplant patients run the risk of falling victim to diseases that might ordinarily be harmless. Roughly half of all transplanted organs become scarred and useless after about five years, having been worn out by their new host's immune systems. Many transplant patients now survive for long enough to need a second and sometimes even a third transplant.

KEY MOMENT

The first kidney transplant

The first successful kidney transplant was carried out from one twin to another in December 1954. The operation was performed by Dr Joseph Murray at Brigham and Women's Hospital, Boston, Massachusetts. No anti-rejection drugs were used. Further kidney transplants between identical twins were carried out immediately afterwards.

Dr Christiaan Barnard who performed the first human heart transplant in 1967.

A quarter of transplanted kidneys come from relatives. This girl was given one of her father's.

Transplanting organs from one person to another opens up more than simply the need for knowledge and expertise. It raises some profound ethical issues as well. Thousands of transplant operations are carried out every year. In about a quarter of kidney transplants a living relative willingly donates the organ. This is only possible because we have two kidneys and can get by with just one. However, the surgery to remove the kidney is painful and the donor may take longer to recover than the person receiving the kidney. Also, the donor is at risk if disease or injury affects the one remaining kidney later in life. Many ethicists believe that it is wrong to require a healthy person to risk a procedure that has no benefit for them and might even cause them harm.

On January 1 1998, the Presumed Organ Donor Law came into effect in Brazil. Under this law anyone's body can be used for organ transplants unless they specifically ask permission to be exempt. Many Brazilian doctors say that the law is a violation of the individual's right to choose. In addition there is a fear among the public that doctors will be pressured into declaring patients brain dead to qualify them as organ donors. Anyone wishing to obtain a non-donor stamp must go through a web of bureaucracy, paying for a new driver's license, national identity card and work document. For the millions of poor and illiterate Brazilians this in effect means that they will have no choice but to give up their organs.

Under present law in Britain, people who are prepared to donate organs put their names on the National Donor Register. However, the families of

OPINION

'If the rich are free to engage in dangerous sports for pleasure, or dangerous jobs for high pay, it is difficult to see why the poor who take the lesser risk of kidney-selling for greater rewards, perhaps saving relatives' lives, or extricating themselves from poverty and debt, should be thought so misguided as to need saving from themselves.'
Medical ethics group, writing in the British medical journal, *The Lancet*, 1998.

potential donors can overrule their decision after death. In December 1998 the British Medical Association's ethics committee approved a plan to allow the organs of any patient who dies in hospital to be removed for transplant without their permission, unless they had chosen to opt out. Michael Wilkes, chairman of the committee, said: 'We have considered the matter and would welcome a move towards legislation for presumed consent. The current situation is that you opt in. We are looking at changing that so people opt out.'

There is an ethical argument for allowing people to sell parts of their bodies on the grounds that the body is a natural asset belonging to the individual and that individuals should be free to make contracts regarding the disposal of their assets. The counter argument is that people are not always in a position to make a free choice. Cases have been reported in countries such as India, Brazil and Egypt of living donors selling kidneys just to make money to get by or to pay off debts. The sale of body parts often exploits those who are most vulnerable. Coercion isn't just applied to people living in poverty. In 1998 a state representative in Missouri, USA, seriously suggested that prisoners awaiting execution be given the option of donating organs in exchange for having their sentence changed to one of life imprisonment.

KEY MOMENT

A black market in organs

In 1995, India's parliament passed a bill limiting organ donations to close relatives and imposing prison terms of up to seven years for selling an organ. The bill was brought in to put a stop to India's thriving underground kidney transplant market. People who needed kidney transplants came to India from Italy, Germany, Yemen, Syria and Turkey, and paid $8,000-$14,000 for the operation. The organs were either purchased from the poor or simply stolen from them. In one province, police claimed to have traced nearly a thousand people whose kidneys were removed without their knowledge by doctors who had asked them to donate blood.

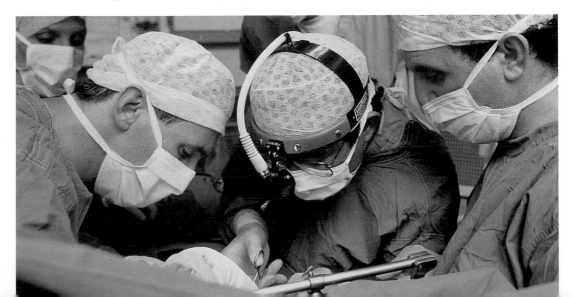

A team of surgeons carry out a liver transplant. Ethical problems arise when someone who has damaged their own liver through alcohol abuse needs a transplant.

One of the most controversial issues involving transplants concerns the use of aborted fetuses. Since it was discovered that fetal tissue could potentially be used in treating Alzheimer's disease, Parkinson's disease and diabetes, as well as some other conditions, it has become highly valued. Anti-abortion activists in the USA mounted a fierce campaign in the mid-1980s when one company began to develop a treatment involving fetal cells.

In 1988 Congress passed an amendment to the US National Organ Transplant Act that extended the act's restrictions to include fetal organs and tissues. This has not stopped the use of fetal parts, however. If it is carried out as part of an approved clinical research program, fetal tissue can still be transplanted into human patients. Although actual sale of the fetal parts is forbidden by law, the agents who obtain them can legally levy a 'handling charge'.

MORE THAN HUMAN?

Because of the problems that surround the use of donated organs from people, research is being carried out into the possible use of organs from other animals. There is great pressure to begin animal transplants because of the acute shortage of available human organs for transplant. Generally only one person out of every three who needs new organs will find a donor. It has

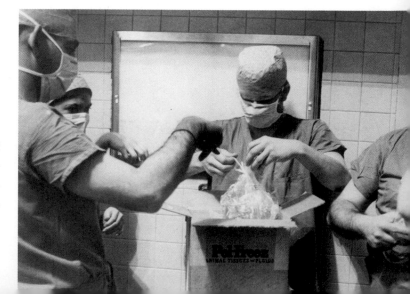

A surgical team unpack a donated kidney to prepare it for transplantation. Kidneys were the first internal organs to be transplanted successfully.

been estimated that if the supply of donated organs were unlimited, four times as many transplants would be carried out each year in the USA alone.

Attempts have been made to transplant organs from baboons or other primates into humans. Huge doses of immunosuppressive drugs are needed to prevent rejection, but this can result in the death of the recipient from infection. The major concern is that animal organs may carry viruses that will be transferred to the human who receives the organ. There is no way to predict whether a virus that is harmless in one species will be harmless in another. Researchers at the University of Alabama showed in 1999 that the most common form of the AIDS virus, human immunodeficiency virus (HIV) type 1, almost certainly passed to humans from chimpanzees. It was concluded that the virus passed from chimps to humans in a small region of western equatorial Africa about fifty years ago. The transmission probably happened when the animals were butchered before being eaten. Over a period of years the virus came into contact with many more hosts, and ultimately became a worldwide problem for which there is, as yet, no cure.

Baboons, which are one candidate for organ donors, carry many viruses, and more are being discovered all the time. Their close relationship to humans increases the chance that their diseases can live in humans. It has been proposed that baboon bone marrow might be transplanted into AIDS patients because baboons do not seem to be susceptible to HIV. The idea is that the damaged immune system of the human is replaced by the healthy baboon immune system. Baboon organs could also be used as a stop-gap for a transplant patient until a human donor could be found. The baboon heart, or whatever, would then be removed and replaced by a human heart. The problem with this is that any viruses that had transferred themselves from the baboon heart would be left behind.

KEY MOMENT

Marissa Ayala

In June 1991, surgeons at the City of Hope National Medical Center in Duarte, California, took bone marrow from fourteen-month-old Marissa Ayala. The marrow was then transplanted into Marissa's nineteen-year-old sister Anissa who was dying from leukemia. The unusual aspect of this story is that a search to find a donor for Anissa had failed. Her best hope was a marrow transplant from a sibling. As the marrow of her brother, Airon, was incompatible, her life depended on a sibling who did not yet exist. First her father had to have his vasectomy surgically reversed, a procedure with a success rate of just forty per cent. Then her mother, Mary, had to become pregnant at the age of forty-three. In April 1990, Marissa was born. The odds were one in four that the baby's bone marrow would match her sister's. There are a number of disturbing ethical issues here. The parents had Marissa as a means of saving another child. The baby, obviously, did not consent to be used in this way. What would the effect be on Marissa when she discovered the reason for her birth? If tests had shown that the tissue of the fetus was not compatible for transplant, would the couple abort the fetus and try again? The Ayalas said they would not, but would this be true in every case?

Using pig parts is potentially a safer proposal. It is now possible to produce humanized organs from pigs that have been genetically engineered so that their tissue doesn't trigger a response from the human immune system. Pigs and humans do have some diseases in common, but in theory pigs could be bred that were free of all known pig diseases. A number of companies, both in Britain and in America, have already been set up to breed pigs especially for organ transplants. Imutran, a biological research company in Britain, is currently compiling a list of all known pig diseases. They are also looking for pig viruses in 160 patients worldwide who have received small portions of pig tissue, such as blood vessel valves. If the results are promising, the company will seek permission to try using a pig liver outside the body as temporary support for a patient awaiting a human organ.

Experiments are being carried out to transplant organs from pigs into monkeys to see if diseases jump from species to species. The trouble is that the transplant 'patients' do not live long enough to be sure that there has been no transfer of disease. In 1995, the Imutran scientists showed that monkeys can survive with genetically-engineered pig organs for more than sixty days. However, some viruses can stay quietly hidden for years before they make their presence felt.

Despite the risks, the transplantation of organs from animals to humans has been given a cautious go-ahead by government, both in the USA and in Britain. The British government circulated a set of national guidelines to hospitals in August 1998. These were intended to ensure that proposed clinical trials don't put patients or the public at risk of new diseases. The guidelines also forbid the use of organs from primates – orang-utans, gorillas and chimpanzees. The UK Xenotransplantation Interim Regulatory Authority (UKXIRA) will regulate animal-to-human transplants. Each application for a clinical trial will be assessed by a panel of experts who will advise the government ministers who make the final decision.

The United States Food and Drug Administration, which has authority to approve all xenotransplantation trials, has called for close monitoring of test results and the creation of a national xenotransplantation advisory committee and a national registry of recipients. Many researchers are convinced that these proposals don't go far enough.

Certainly what has been called the 'yuck factor' has to be taken into account when considering xenotransplants. For many people, the pig is an unclean animal and their religious beliefs would be strongly against pig to human transplants. However, there are good reasons for choosing the pig. Its organs grow to about the same size as a human's and can therefore be more readily transplanted. Just as importantly it is a domesticated animal that we have been accustomed to make use of for centuries. Using organs for transplant rather than food would be just one more use to which the pig can be put. It is hard to mount an ethical objection to pig transplants while you happily eat a pork chop.

For many, the use of animals as a source of organs for humans is morally unacceptable, as is their use for any medical research.

A GOOD DEATH

All of us will die some day – that much is certain. Although we look to medicine to delay our final day, we do not necessarily wish for continued life for as long as possible under any circumstances. The extended span of life that modern medicine can bring comes with a price-tag attached. That price might be seeing loved ones lingering on in pain, or having their bodies kept alive after the loss of their personalities through brain damage. If such suffering is all that life has to offer, some people may want to choose death rather than life. Sometimes, indeed, people look to medicine not to prolong life, but to end it.

The moral and ethical issues that surround death are quite as profound as those that concern life's beginnings. Life is held to be sacred by some people and suicide, the voluntary ending of one's own life, is frowned upon as an immoral act. For others, the issue of when to die and the right to choose your own time is a matter of individual freedom.

TERMINAL CARE

For most people in the western world death usually comes in advanced age, perhaps at the end of a long illness. For many, this means dying in hospital or a nursing home. Inevitably death, like birth, has come to be seen as an event to be managed by health-care professionals. Like birth, however, the technology surrounding death in hospitals can be a cause of concern for many people, who worry that they or their relatives might be kept alive long after there is any hope of improvement in their quality of life. There is a fear that the patient becomes simply a battleground on which the doctors fight against death. In New Jersey, USA in 1976, the Karen Ann Quinlan case was among the first to bring issues such as this to public attention. Karen was involved in an accident which left her in a deep coma, showing no signs of consciousness; she was kept alive by means of a respirator and a feeding tube. Her parents, after consulting their Catholic priest, wanted her to be allowed to die but they were forced to take the matter to court to win the right to have the respirator disconnected.

Dr Cicely Saunders in England, Dr Elizabeth Kübler-Ross in the USA and Dr Balfour Mount of the Royal Victoria Hospital in Montréal have pioneered the setting up of hospices, which specialize in providing care for the terminally ill. In 1967, St Christopher's Hospice, the first of its kind, was founded by Cicely Saunders in London. There the emphasis is on providing high-quality care, including adequate pain control and emotional support for patients who realize that they are dying. In contrast to a hospital, the hospice staff are encouraged to form an emotional commitment to the patients and recognize the needs of relatives and other close friends. Dr Saunders said: 'The care of the dying demands all that we can do to enable patients to live until they die.'

> **KEY MOMENT**
>
> **On Death and Dying**
> In 1969, Elizabeth Kübler-Ross, one of the pioneers of the hospice movement, published *On Death and Dying*, one of the first books to encourage open discussion about coming to terms with death.

Care in a hospice focuses on maintaining the quality of life for the terminally ill patient.

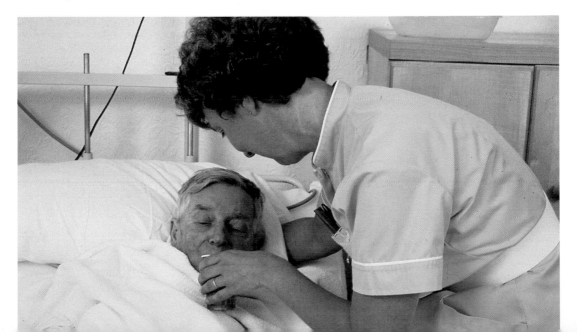

Mercy killing or murder?

By his own admission, the controversial American physician Dr Jack Kevorkian, 'Dr Death' to the media, had attended the suicides of twenty-eight seriously ill people since 1990. At the end of November 1998 Kevorkian was charged with first-degree murder by Oakland County, Michigan prosecutor David Gorcyca. In a bizarre gesture, Kevorkian had provided the evidence for his prosecution. On 17 September 1998 he had videotaped himself administering a lethal injection to a terminally ill man, Thomas Youk, who wished to die. The tape was televised across the USA on the CBS news show *60 Minutes* on 22 November 1998. Gorcyca said that Kevorkian's actions clearly fitted the definition of premeditated murder and that Youk's consent was not a valid legal defence. Kevorkian has said that if he is sent to prison he will starve himself. He was found guilty of the lesser charge of second degree murder on 26 March 1999.

THE TIME OF DEATH

Thanks to the sophisticated life-support equipment now available to hospitals, it is possible to keep alive people who not so many decades ago would have simply died. When machines control a patient's heartbeat and breathing and there is no trace of any activity in the brain, is that person alive or dead? Like the debate that surrounds the rights and wrongs of abortion, the issue here is surely what it means to be a person. For many, particularly those with religious beliefs, it can be a question of balancing the desire to preserve life if at all possible with the quality of that life.

When the brain is no longer functioning and the personality has disappeared, is it right simply to keep the body going artificially? Is there a point on some sliding scale of brain function at which we can say this person is dead? Almost certainly there isn't, nor is it likely that there ever will be. To take just two examples: Karen Ann Quinlan continued to live for nearly ten years after doctors switched off her respirator in 1976. No one had expected that she

Euthanasia is illegal in Britain and members of the pressure group Exit have been prosecuted.

would go on breathing for herself, although she never did emerge from her coma. And in June 1998, a young woman who had been in a prolonged coma following an accident suddenly regained consciousness. Doctors had decided not to replace her feeding tube, which had fallen out, and were just about to turn off her ventilator when she awoke.

Another problem faced by doctors and the relatives of the patient is that organs could perhaps be removed from the patient for transplantation, giving life to someone else. In Italy, doctors are already using patients in a persistent vegetative state for organ donation. In the USA, doctors are considering taking organs from anencephalic children, those rare cases of babies who are born with part of their brain not developed.

EUTHANASIA

In March 1998, an elderly woman who was dying of breast cancer became the first person to commit legal, doctor-assisted suicide under the state of Oregon's Death with Dignity Act, which came into effect in November 1997. Others soon followed. The director of the Connecticut Hospice believed that many terminally ill patients were afraid of the effect the Oregon law might have on care for the dying. They felt safer in hospices where euthanasia was not practised.

In Britain, the Voluntary Euthanasia Society was set up in 1935 to campaign for people's right to die at a time of their choosing. In 1997 membership stood at 20,000, most of whom were women of sixty or over – many of them having nursed their husbands through the final stages of illness.

> **OPINION**
>
> 'A competent, terminally-ill adult, having lived nearly the full measure of his life, has a strong liberty interest in choosing a dignified and humane death rather than being reduced at the end of his existence to a childlike state of helplessness, diapered, sedated, incompetent.'
> Judge Stephen Reinhardt, overturning Washington state's ban on doctor-assisted suicide, 1996.

Dr Jack Kevorkian (centre), a strong advocate of euthanasia, was shown assisting the suicide of a terminally ill man on national television in the USA in November 1998.

OPINION

'I never want to have to wonder whether the physician coming into my hospital room is wearing the white coat of the healer... or the black hood of the executioner. Trust between patient and physician is simply too important and too fragile to be subjected to the unnecessary strain.'
Alexander Capron, American lawyer.

In 1980, Derek Humphry founded the Hemlock Society in the USA. The society's charter states that one of its aims 'is to promote a climate of public opinion which is tolerant of the right of people who are terminally ill to end their own lives in a planned manner.' In 1991 the Hemlock Society published a controversial book called *Final Exit*, which contained detailed instructions on how people could take their own lives. The book was condemned as a suicide manual and there was evidence that it had been consulted by people who were not terminally ill but had committed suicide for other reasons. It sold over a million copies.

In the Netherlands, in 1971, a doctor who admitted administering a lethal dose of morphine was given a one-year suspended sentence, a lenient decision that sparked a public debate. In 1984 the Royal Dutch Medical Association set out guidelines to help the courts decide at what point euthanasia becomes a crime. These were accepted by the Ministry of Justice in 1990 and in 1993 the Dutch parliament finally voted in favour of the recommendations. Medical colleges in the Netherlands have accepted the doctor's right to intervene at the patient's request to bring about death under certain circumstances. Often, however, the rules of conduct appear to be disregarded and there are frequent cases of doctors performing active euthanasia without the explicit consent of the patient, or administering overdoses of pain-controlling drugs without

Dr Philip Nitschke designed computer software that assisted terminally ill patients in committing suicide by allowing them to control a lethal injection. The software was designed for use in Australia's Northern Territories when that state passed a law, later overturned by the Australian parliament, that permitted euthanasia.

the patient's knowledge. In 1995, 900 patients were reported to have died as a result of a doctor performing euthanasia without it being requested. Twenty-three per cent of doctors said that they had ended a patient's life without his or her explicit request. More than 10,000 people in the Netherlands now carry 'declaration of life' cards because they fear being killed by doctors who are over-enthusiastic about euthanasia.

In Britain, euthanasia remains illegal, although Dr Nigel Cox, a GP who admitted giving a lethal dose of a drug to a patient in 1992, is still practising after receiving a suspended sentence in court and a reprimand from the General Medical Council. In Australia, parliament overturned a law that permitted euthanasia in that country's Northern Territories.

The difficult decisions that have to be made when someone is close to death have been eased somewhat by the development of 'living wills', in which people set out their wishes for how far they would wish their treatment to be taken. In 1983, the Natural Death Act made these living wills legally binding documents in South Australia. Living will and other health-care advance directives have legal force in practically all states of the USA, although perhaps only fifteen per cent of people will file one.

In hospitals in the United States, medical staff or relatives of the patients can ask for a consultation with a bioethicist. In a private meeting with those concerned, the bioethicist learns about the patient's illness and beliefs and wishes, and discusses how each person sees their ethical obligations. The bioethicist might gather all the interested parties together to talk about the situation. If this group session doesn't resolve the issue, the ethicist will conduct an official review and make formal recommendations as to what should be done.

OPINION

'There is much pressure on doctors to practise euthanasia. Up to now a doctor who did not want to carry out euthanasia could say that it was against the law, but now it will be the right of the patient to request it. It will be part of the job of the doctor. We are going into a new area and we don't know where it will end. It is a total change in the role of the doctor if killing patients becomes part of the job.'
Dr Krijn Haasnood, Dutch Physicians Association spokesman, 1998.

OF SOUND MIND

It is a startling fact that nearly half of the hospital beds in western countries are occupied by people with psychiatric disorders. A definition of mental health that would satisfy everyone is not easy. It may be downright impossible. Perhaps the best we can say is that mental health is having all the abilities and attitudes that allow us to function within society. Cultures and societies at different times and in different places have come up with diverse ideas about what constitutes acceptable behaviour. Anyone who does not observe or conform to the normal standards of their society runs the risk of being considered mentally ill, or worse, by those who do not share their views.

Patients in mental hospitals at the beginning of the twentieth century received little in the way of treatment or understanding of their illnesses.

The branch of medicine that deals with the causes and treatment of mental diseases is called psychiatry, a word that comes from two Greek words meaning 'mind' and 'healing'. It was really only in the twentieth century that psychiatry came to be seen as a respectable science. Even today most people would be ashamed to admit that they or someone close to them was seeing a psychiatrist. We can still hear people with mental illnesses called 'lunatics', 'psychos' and 'oddballs', proof, perhaps, of the hostility that people who consider themselves 'normal' feel for those they consider to be 'different'.

The treatment of mental disorders is an ethical minefield – not least because of the difficulty in defining what actually constitutes a 'disorder'. In the nineteenth century the philosophy of *mens sana in corpore sano* – a healthy mind in a healthy body – meant, as the writer T C Clouston put it in 1906, a refusal even to admit 'the possibility of a healthy mind in an unsound body'.

The study of the mind and its illnesses has been strongly influenced by the ideas of the Austrian doctor Sigmund Freud, who believed that our conscious mental lives are determined by unconscious ideas, impulses and emotions. In the last years of the nineteenth century, Freud developed a method he called psychical analysis (later, psychoanalysis). This involved interpreting, or analyzing, what the patient says when told to report his or her thoughts. In 1900 Freud published *The Interpretation of Dreams* in which he applied psychoanalysis to the study of dreams. He sought to demonstrate that disorders in the brain could be explained as a result of past experiences. Psychoanalysis did not become widely known in Britain until the 1920s.

Sigmund Freud (1856-1939) was the founder of psychoanalysis and a major influence on the way people approached the subject of mental illness.

Psychoanalysis generally takes place over a period of two to three years, involving several sessions a week with a therapist. It is therefore a rather expensive form of treatment and available only to relatively few people. Little hard and fast research has been done into the effectiveness of its methods which rely on the therapist's interpretation of the patient's statements.

OPINION

'For patients who are frustrated by disappointing events in their lives but who are still able to function adequately... skilled psychotherapy should be energetically and adequately administered.... ECT... can neither remove nor resolve life-situational problems.'
Massachusetts Journal of Mental Health, 1973.

ECT

Electroconvulsive therapy (ECT, also known as electroshock therapy) involves giving electric shocks to the brain to induce convulsions that appear to have a beneficial effect on patients suffering from disorders such as depression. The curative possibilities of these treatments were discovered in the 1930s by Italian psychiatrists Ugo Cerletti and Lucio Bini. The patient is first anaesthetized and made unconscious for several minutes. A muscle relaxant is also given. An electric current lasting from a half to a few seconds is passed through the brain between two electrodes applied to the scalp. This produces a seizure that lasts from thirty seconds to a minute. After the treatment the patient feels confused and disorientated, but this clears within several minutes to several hours. A series of treatments, usually given three times a week, is necessary to relieve the patient's symptoms. Treatment is often then continued with anti-depressant medication. Unlike drugs, ECT produces results immediately.

In the 1950s, many doctors saw ECT as potentially useful for a wide range of disorders, in particular chronic depression. ECT research during the 1960s focused on attempts to understand how it worked but the results were inconclusive. In the 1970s, increasing concerns with the rights of the patient prompted a closer examination of ECT. An influential report published in the *Massachusetts Journal of Mental Health* in 1973 found that most authorities were in agreement that depression was treated effectively by ECT, but that there was no agreement as to its worth in treating other conditions.

There was general agreement that informed consent prior to ECT was essential. If the person was unable to grant consent, a relative or guardian should be found to take responsibility. There was unanimous agreement that 'administration of ECT to children...

has no established usefulness and that therefore such treatment on a routine basis cannot be justified'.

Little was known about how ECT worked and there was increasing concern about its safety and possible side effects. It was seen as hazardous and irreversible. An Alabama state judge ruled in the 1970s that before ECT could be administered (even when consent had been obtained), confirmation from four psychiatrists and one neurologist, as well as monitoring by two attorneys, was required. By the end of the 1970s, a second, independent psychiatric opinion was required in Britain whenever ECT was considered for compulsorily detained persons.

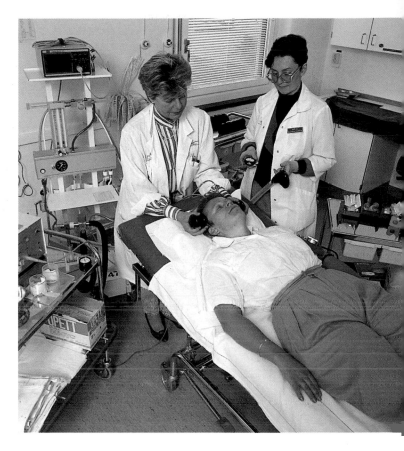

A patient is prepared for electroshock therapy in a clinic in Sweden. Great care is taken to ensure that the patient comes to no harm when the shock is administered.

At the beginning of the 1980s, ECT was being used to treat people with severe mood disorder, sleep disturbance, loss of appetite, feelings of guilt and some other disorders. Risks identified included the risk of heart attack or brain haemorrhage during treatment. A *British Journal of Psychiatry* report in 1983 stated the importance of obtaining consent. A full explanation, including information about risks and side effects, should be given to the client. Consent should always precede ECT treatment, and could be withdrawn at any stage. Next of kin or other close relatives were not allowed to give consent and had no legal right to give consent on behalf of another person.

Frances Farmer

In 1948 Walter Freeman performed his most famous trans-orbital lobotomy when he operated on Frances Farmer, a thirty-four-year-old film star and political activist. Farmer had rebelled all her life against every form of authority, and despite her success as an actress, found herself committed to Western State Hospital in Fort Stellacoombe, Washington. Farmer seemed resistant to all forms of therapy and finally the decision was taken to perform a lobotomy on her. In October Walter Freeman arrived at the hospital where he was scheduled to perform a number of lobotomies. After a brief talk to an assembly of hospital staff and visiting psychiatrists on the usefulness of lobotomy and its potential to control society's misfits, Freeman set to work. Patient after patient was shocked into a faint by having electrodes placed on their temples. Then Freeman lifted an eyelid and plunged his icepick into the patient's head. Perhaps because of her celebrity status, Frances Farmer was at least granted the dignity of having her lobotomy performed in a private room. Her rebellious personality was effectively destroyed that day. She never resumed her career in movies and ended her life as a clerk in a hotel.

PSYCHOSURGERY

The surgical cutting of brain tissue to disconnect one part of the brain from the other, or the removal or destruction of brain tissue altogether for the purpose of altering behaviour, is called psychosurgery. It has been used to treat, amongst other things, anxiety and depression, obsessive and compulsive behaviour, aggressiveness and drug addiction and other psychiatric disorders.

Psychosurgery was first developed in Portugal in 1935, and soon spread to the USA and Britain. American scientist Carlyle Jacobsen performed an operation on aggressive chimpanzees that made them more docile without affecting their intelligence or co-ordination. Jacobsen surgically destroyed a part of each animal's frontal lobe, a section of the outer part of the brain. He called the operation a lobotomy. Egaz Moniz, a Portuguese neuropsychiatrist, performed lobotomies on twenty mental patients. He reported that seven were cured, eight improved, and five unimproved. In 1936 neurologist Walter Freeman and neurosurgeon James Watts took the technique to the USA, where

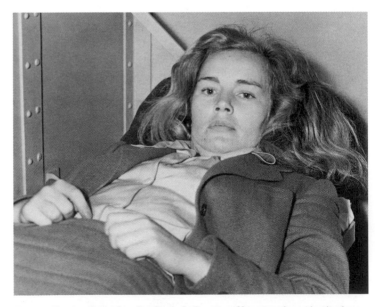

Frances Farmer pictured on her bunk during one of her stays in an institution.

Egaz Moniz, one of the pioneers of psychosurgery. In 1949 he was awarded the Nobel prize for his work.

the operation was greeted as a major breakthrough in the treatment of the mentally ill.

The actual procedure Freeman developed was like something from a horror movie. Using a small mallet, Freeman would drive an ice pick through the eye socket, then move it around inside the skull, destroying large volumes of brain tissue. At one point Freeman travelled around the USA on what he called 'headhunting' expeditions, performing ice-pick lobotomies on thousands of unfortunate patients.

The operation had many unfortunate side effects, including personality changes, impairment of judgement, and the loss of creativity and intellectual ability. As many as 50,000 operations were performed in the USA up to the mid-1950s, most of them on schizophrenic patients. Psychosurgery fell from favour with the introduction of tranquillizers and other drugs that were used to treat mental illness. At the same time, growing evidence suggested that patients who had had psychosurgery performed on them showed no real improvement.

KEY MOMENT

Sweden's lobotomies scandal

In 1998, the Swedish authorities faced huge claims for compensation when it emerged that, in an officially approved program that lasted for almost twenty years, up to 4,500 mental patients had been forced to undergo lobotomies against their will. Many were psychiatric patients whose relatives had not been asked for permission to operate, as required by law. Others included children classified as 'developmentally impaired'. Swedish MP Dan Ericsson said: 'It's quite extraordinary that parliament has been so indifferent to this dreadful affair in the past.' He accused successive Swedish governments and senior civil servants of covering up information on potentially controversial issues. 'I'm convinced people are ready to confront the ghosts from Sweden's recent history, but there is still no climate of openness in high places here,' he said.

Psychosurgery raises a number of ethical issues involving the rights of the patient, the performing of experiments on humans, the right of the physician to attempt to control the behaviour of another person. There is the risk that psychosurgery may be used to remove from society those people who are, for whatever reason, 'awkward' to have around. There have been a number of attempts by governments, the medical professions and others involved with patient rights to establish guidelines and safeguards for psychosurgery. Opponents of psychosurgery point to the fact that it is irreversible, for one thing.

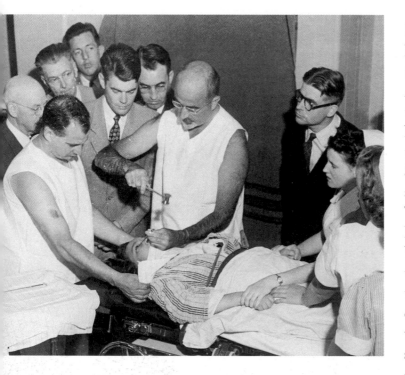

Walter Freeman performing a lobotomy while nurses and students look on.

In 1974 the National Research Act was passed in the USA. With this Act, Congress authorized the establishment of a National Commission for the Protection of Human Subjects of Biomedical and Behavioral Research. The National Institute of Mental Health in the USA has recommended that psychosurgery is treated as an experimental therapy, with all the special safeguards and consideration for patients' rights that apply to any experimental procedures. However, many argue that psychosurgery should be viewed as a routine treatment for a number of behavioural problems.

The number of patients actually receiving psychosurgical treatment is relatively small. A large American hospital might perform only twenty operations in a year. Only patients who are at high risk for suicide, for example, and can prove that they've tried every other form of therapy and drug treatment available will be offered surgery. Unlike in Walter Freeman's time, no operation is performed today without the patient's informed consent.

A CHEMICAL SOLUTION?

Researchers believe that some mood disorders, such as depression, result from imbalances of certain chemicals in the brain called neurotransmitters. These allow the nerve cells in the brain to communicate with each other by means of electrical impulses. Bipolar disorder, sometimes called manic-depression, occurs in several forms, the most common of which is a period of mania followed by one of depression. The neurotransmitters that appear to be involved in bipolar disorder are norepinephrine, serotonin and dopamine. It has been discovered that certain drugs can affect the balance of these brain chemicals. In 1949 Australian psychiatrist John Cade gave lithium salt to a fifty-one-year-old mental patient. This man was so manic-depressive and uncontrollable that he had spent twenty years of his life locked up in asylums. After less than a week of lithium, his mood swings were gone and he was a normal, functioning human being. Within three months he was back in his own home.

A psychiatric patient is encouraged to talk through his problems and is helped to interpret them by an analyst.

The FDA approved lithium as a drug in 1969 after safe doses had been established (it is toxic in large amounts). Lithium is the most effective medicine yet discovered for bipolar disorder. Symptoms disappear in seventy per cent of manic bipolar patients within four to ten days. It is not a cure, and

must be used indefinitely (usually with psychotherapy) to prevent the return of symptoms. It is not certain if the treatment actually stops the mood swings or whether it simply dampens down the highs and lows felt by the sufferer. Most researchers seem to think that it depends on the individual.

The problem with the chemical solution to mental problems was that inevitably people began to look for quick fixes. If the brain was to be seen as a machine, albeit an astoundingly complex one, then it could be fixed when it went wrong. Feeling bad? Take a pill.

One of the wonder drugs of the 1990s was Prozac, a seemingly low risk antidote for depression. In the USA Prozac, as well as being prescribed for adults, is prescribed to children, the elderly and even pets. Over half a million prescriptions for Prozac-type drugs were written out for children of five and over in the USA in one year. Many question the desirability of offering Prozac to children as no one knows how it, and drugs like it, might affect a growing child. They see the trend towards giving pills, such as Prozac for depression and Ritalin for hyperactivity to children as an unethical practice. Health-care workers point out the obvious problems that arise when, on the one hand children are being told to 'say no' to drugs, while on the other hand their parents are being offered Prozac and Ritalin to make the children's behaviour more 'normal'.

The idea of normal behaviour and changing the personality lies at the centre of the ethical problems that arise from manipulating the mind. An important question to ask is this: is the person who emerges from psychoanalysis, brain surgery or a course of drugs the same person as he or she was at the beginning? Ethically it is possible to argue that the original personality is being dismantled, and a new personality is being put in its place.

BRAVE NEW WORLD?

At the heart of the cells that make up our bodies is a remarkable molecule called DNA. All the information and instructions that the cells need to grow and function is contained within their DNA. These instructions come in the form of genes – a length of DNA that has the code for making a particular protein necessary either for body structure or for carrying out the chemical processes that go on in the body.

In the 1980s, scientists began work on a massive undertaking – to label and decode all of the human genetic code, or human genome. The plan is to identify all of the estimated 50,000 to 100,000 human genes by the year 2005. It is reckoned that there are around three billion chemical code letters making up these genes, so it is a mammoth task. Some people see the Human Genome Project, as it is called, as one of the most important undertakings ever attempted, comparing it with the Manhattan Project to develop the atomic bomb during the Second World War.

Once a gene has been located and its sequence of chemical code letters has been unravelled, tests can be devised for the presence of that gene. A number of the genes already identified are those with defects, which can cause illnesses in any patient. Among the many tests available are those for genetic disorders such as cystic fibrosis, Huntington's disease, muscular dystrophy, neurofibromatosis and retinoblastoma.

OPINION

'We are gaining the power to intervene in a realm that we've never had access to... by introducing new genes into the flow from one generation to another. Some people say you can't do that, you shouldn't do that. But I think we just have to take responsibility and move forward.'
Gregory Stock, director of the program on science, technology and society at the University of California at Los Angeles, 1998.

Laboratory testing of DNA has given us the ability to detect the presence of genes that may cause defects or illnesses.

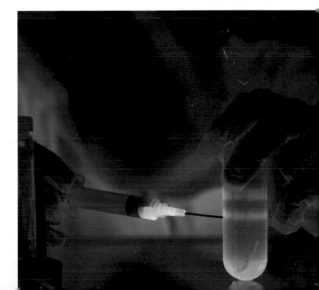

KEY MOMENT

Disease-free mice

In an experiment carried out in the early 1980s, Leroy Hood and colleagues at the California Institute of Technology added genes to mouse embryos that had an inherited nervous system disorder. The new genes got into all the embryo cells – including those that later developed into sperm and eggs. Not only were the mice born free of disease, but all their offspring were as well.

Before the cystic fibrosis test was developed, to take one example, people with instances of this disease in their families faced a dilemma. This life-threatening disease occurs in individuals who have inherited two cystic fibrosis genes, one from each parent. By the laws of genetics, any offspring of two carriers has a one in four chance of inheriting two genes and falling ill with the disorder. They also have a one in four chance of inheriting no cystic fibrosis gene at all. The test gives prospective parents the chance to know whether they are carriers and what the risks are in having children. A technique is being developed that will enable doctors to grow fertilized eggs in the laboratory and test their DNA for genetic disorders, like cystic fibrosis. If the embryo is found to be healthy it can then be implanted in the woman's uterus and the pregnancy can proceed.

David B Weiner is one of a team of researchers developing vaccines that trigger the immune system by introducing a segment of viral DNA into the body.

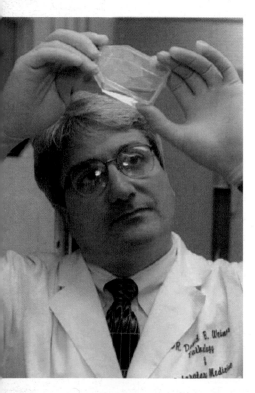

GENE THERAPY

Many medical researchers see gene therapy as the answer to gene-based disease. Ashanthi DeSilva was born with a rare, inherited disorder called ADA deficiency in which a faulty gene meant that her immune system did not function properly. She was vulnerable to a host of common diseases, some of which could have been fatal. Treatment with drugs wasn't working and researchers at the US National Institutes of Health proposed a bold experiment. In September 1990, a team led by doctors W French Anderson and R Michael Blaese extracted T cells, part of her immune system, from Ashanthi and exposed them to mouse leukemia viruses into which human ADA genes had been spliced. The viruses, which had been made harmless, invaded the T cells and carried the ADA gene with them into the T cell DNA. Finally, the T cells, many of them now newly fitted with a working ADA gene, were dripped back into Ashanthi's veins.

Over the next two years this procedure was repeated until the level of ADA in her bloodstream was twenty-five per cent of normal, more than enough to give protection from disease. As a precaution she continued to receive weekly doses of drug treatment alongside the gene treatments. Periodic tests have confirmed that the re-engineered cells are surviving and continuing to produce ADA. Anderson concedes that Ashanthi's gene therapy has not produced a cure, because the T cells made by her bone marrow still lack a working ADA gene. He insists, however, that 'Ashi does provide proof of the principle that if you put a correct gene into enough cells in a patient, you will correct the disease.'

The experimental procedure that saved Ashanthi DeSilva was controversial. It was viewed as tampering with the human genetic code, and the team were only given permission to conduct the experiment after they gave assurances that the genetic change would not be passed on to any children Ashanthi might have.

Researchers are now exploring another kind of gene therapy that could prove to be far more contentious. The goal is to reprogram the germline cells – the sperm or egg cells – a technique that would allow the removal of unwanted genes and change the genetic make-up of a person's unborn descendants.

> **KEY MOMENT**
>
> **Artificial chromosomes**
> In 1997 scientists announced that they had invented artificial human chromosomes – miniature, synthetic chromosomes complete with one or more genes. These chromosomes make themselves at home inside cells, and they divide each time the cell divides, just like real chromosomes do. No artificial chromosomes have been inserted into living people's cells yet, but several scientists believe they may be ideal for germline gene therapy.

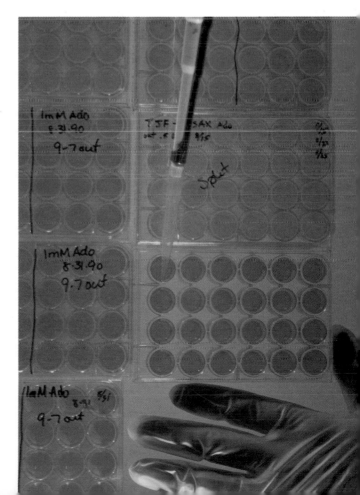

Growing genetically-corrected cell cultures. Gene therapy employs viruses to carry vital genes into the cells of someone who lacks them.

OPINION

'As with cloning, there are real concerns about whether we are wise enough to mold ourselves to the extent these technologies may allow us to mold ourselves. It certainly makes me nervous.'
Erik Parens, ethicist at the Hastings Center, Garrison, New York, 1998.

A major problem with germline gene therapy is that no one understands the complex ways in which genes interact. Wiping out a disease gene could have unforeseen side effects. For example, people who have inherited only one copy of the gene for sickle cell anemia are not ill but are protected against malaria. Similarly people who carry one copy of the gene that causes cystic fibrosis are protected against cholera. No one knows what would happen if all 'disease genes' were removed. More worryingly, any mistake the gene therapist made would become fixed in the patient's genetic make-up to be passed to the next generation, with possibly catastrophic consequences.

The USA, Canada, Britain and some other countries forbid germline gene therapy at present, but may reconsider in the future. Dr W French Anderson believes that germline gene therapy is sure to come, because 'no parent will willingly pass on lethal genes to their children if they can prevent it.' A major ethical problem to overcome may be that of consent – there is no way, after all, that future generations can agree to the alteration of their genes.

Genetic tests could also be used by employers and insurance companies to identify people who might be occupational or insurance risks. People carrying genes that put

In microbiology laboratories such as this around the world, techniques are being developed to manipulate DNA and influence the development of humans from the earliest stages.

them at risk of developing a life-threatening disease or a behavioural disorder could find themselves being discriminated against. If there was a possibility that you were carrying a defective gene, would you necessarily want to know about it?

CLONING

In 1997, the world met Dolly the sheep. Dolly looked just like any other sheep, but she was rather special. Researchers at the Roslin Institute in Scotland had extracted cells from the udder of an adult ewe. Then they had removed the nucleus, the part of the cell that contains the genetic material, from another sheep's unfertilized egg. A cell from the first sheep's udder, with its own DNA, was then joined to the egg with electricity to make it start growing into an embryo. The embryo was then transplanted into the uterus of another ewe that acted as Dolly's surrogate mother. Dolly contains the same genetic information as the ewe that provided the udder cells. She is a clone of the first sheep.

The creation of Dolly had an extraordinary effect. Religious leaders and many ethicists were concerned by this development. The Vatican condemned it immediately as an unnatural practice. The British government announced an end to the Roslin Institute's funding. Many people called for international ethical safeguards against the potential abuses of biotechnology. The Roslin researchers became the targets of animal rights activists. The Institute was overwhelmed with appeals from people around the world who wanted the team to recreate dead loved ones. Of course, there is more to the development of human beings than their genes. Environment plays a crucial role. Even if human cloning was successfully carried out, there would be no way to recreate the experiences that shaped the original person.

OPINION

'Every child should be wanted for itself, as an individual. In making a copy of oneself or some famous person, a parent is deliberately specifying the way he or she wishes that child to develop. In recent years, particularly in the US, much importance has been placed on the right of individuals to reproduce in ways that they wish. I suggest that there is a greater need to consider the interests of the child and to reject these proposed uses of cloning.'
Dr Ian Wilmut, Roslin Institute, 1999.

Dolly the sheep was the first mammal to be successfully cloned. The cloning of human embryos, however, raises a host of ethical problems.

'We may be rushing into something we don't understand very well. Some people have the belief that embryos are human just like you and me. We don't want to industrialize embryo production.'
Tom Murray, director of the Center for Biomedical Ethics, Case Western University, Ohio, 1999.

KEY MOMENT

Transgenic animals
In 1987, transgenic mice were produced that made a human enzyme in their milk that helps to dissolve blood clots. Since then, human proteins have been obtained from the milk of sheep, goats and cows.

In January 1999 Dr Ian Wilmut, head of the Roslin Institute, announced plans to embark on a human embryo-cloning project aimed at treating conditions such as diabetes and Parkinson's disease. The planned research would not result in cloning complete human beings. The team would clone human embryos, withdraw cells known as stem cells – cells capable of developing into any tissue type – and discard the rest. Stem cells can be used to generate healthy new cells that can be used in the treatment of some diseases. Also in that month the National Institutes of Health in the USA announced it would grant federal funding for research on laboratory-grown stem cells because they do not constitute an embryo. Federally-funded research on actual embyros would still be forbidden.

MAKING MONSTERS

In the 1990s, scientists at the University of Texas and at the University of Bath created, respectively, headless mice and headless tadpoles. Researchers found the gene that tells the embryo to produce the head, and then deleted it. Four mice embryos manipulated in this way were born. Having no way to breathe, the mice died instantly. So what are the reasons for this form of experimentation? Using the same techniques, it would almost certainly be possible to produce human bodies without higher brain functions. These bodies would have no consciousness and could not, legally, be considered persons. It would therefore be possible to keep them alive simply as sources of organs for transplantation.

Combined with cloning, the potential exists to create a headless twin of a person who could provide them with replacements for their diseased organs. Each transplant would be precisely matched to the recipient, and there would be no possibility of rejection and no need for immunosuppressant drugs.

There are obvious and serious ethical difficulties with these proposals. Many people would find the idea of creating headless humans repellent. But is this a good enough reason to turn our backs on a technique that could ultimately save lives? For centuries we have been manipulating life in one way or another, selecting those animals and plants that provide us with the qualities we seek. Are we ready now to start manipulating ourselves? A survey carried out by the American Medical Association in 1997 showed that an overwhelming number of people are seriously worried by medical ethics issues such as advances in genetic engineering, doctor-assisted suicide and euthanasia, and the quality of health-care available.

During the course of the twentieth century, scientific discoveries and developments have progressed at a rapid pace. There is no reason to think that the pace will slow down in the twenty-first century, indeed it will probably speed up. The difficulty for the ethicist lies in coming to terms with the unforeseen, and unforeseeable, consequences of those developments.

OPINION

'I have no sleepless nights. I fully understand that there are people who find this all deeply offensive.'
Ian Wilmut, head of the Roslin Institute team.

The mouse on the right has been genetically engineered to be more muscular than a normal mouse. This experiment may be helpful in finding a cure for muscular dystrophy.

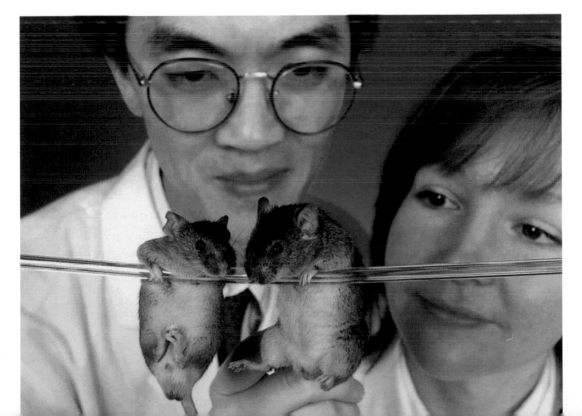

GLOSSARY

abortion bringing about the end of a pregnancy by removing the fetus from the womb before it is capable of survival.

anaesthesia loss of sensation brought about by administering an anaesthetic and thereby allowing pain-free surgery to be performed.

antibiotics substances produced by or obtained from certain bacteria or fungi that can be used to kill or inhibit the growth of disease-causing microbes. Penicillin was the first antibiotic to be discovered.

bacteria plural of bacterium, members of one of the great kingdoms of the living world. Bacteria are tiny single-celled organisms found everywhere; some are disease agents but many are an essential part of the natural world, contributing to the decomposition of wastes for example.

biochemicals chemical substances occuring in and produced by living organisms.

chromosomes structures that become visible in a cell when it divides. Chromosomes are where the genes, the units of heredity, are located.

compound a substance that contains atoms of two or more elements joined together chemically.

contraception deliberate prevention of pregnancy by a physical barrier or chemical or surgical interference with natural fertility.

embryo an organism in the early stages of development from the fertilization of the egg until it reaches a recognizable form.

euthanasia the deliberate ending of someone's life to relieve them of the pain of an incurable condition.

fetus the unborn child after the eighth week of pregnancy when it has taken on the basic appearance of a developed human.

hormones substances produced in one part of the body and transported via the bloodstream to another part where they produce an effect, such as growth. Hormones are sometimes called chemical messengers.

menopause the time at which a woman ceases to produce an egg every month, usually between the ages of 45 and 55, and can no longer become pregnant.

micro-organism an organism that is too small to be seen with the naked eye, such as a bacterium or an amoeba, and can, as the name suggests, only be seen using a microscope.

pharmaceutical of or relating to pharmacy, the act of preparing and dispensing drugs for medical purposes.

physician someone who practices medicine, a medical doctor.

radiation energy emitted in the form of particles or waves. High energy radiation can cause damage to living tissue.

radioactive giving off energy in the form of radiation.

schizophrenic suffering from schizophrenia, one of a group of mental disorders characterized by withdrawal from reality, delusions, hallucinations and other symptoms.

sedative a drug that has a soothing or calming effect, used to relieve stress or anxiety.

synthesize to combine two or more things to produce something more complex.

transgenic describing an organism that carries genes that have been transferred to it from another species.

vaccine a preparation of a weakened or killed disease-causing bacterium or virus that stimulates the body's defence mechanisms without causing full-blown disease symptoms and thereby gives protection when the active disease agent is encountered.

ventilator a device, also called a respirator, that helps an ill person to breathe.

virus the simplest form of life, many times smaller than a bacterium; viruses are often disease-causing agents.

xenotransplantation transplantation of organs from one species to another, such as from a pig to a human.

BOOKS TO READ

Abortion: Opposing Viewpoints by Tamara L Roleff, Greenhaven Press, 1996.

Am I My Brother's Keeper? by Arthur L Caplan, Indiana University Press, 1998.

Bioethics and High-tech Medicine by Victoria Sherrow, Twenty-First Century Books, 1996.

Bioethics and the New Medical Technology by Margot C J Mabie, Atheneum Books, 1993.

Medical Ethics: Moral and Legal Conflicts in Health Care by Daniel Jussim, J Messner, 1990.

Medical Ethics Today, British Medical Association, 1993.

Pregnancy: Private Decisions, Public Debates by Kathlyn Gay, Franklin Watts, 1994.

A Right to Die? by Richard Walker, Franklin Watts, 1997.

The Right to Die: Public Controversy, Private Matter by Kathlyn Gay, Franklin Watts, 1993.

WEBSITES

Bioethics for Beginners
http://www.med.upenn.edu/~bioethic/outreach/bioforbegin/index1.html

Bulletin of Medical Ethics
http://www.ourworld.compuserve.com/homepages/Bulletin-of-Medical-Ethics

Center for Bioethics Virtual Library
http://www.med.upenn.edu/~bioethic/library/

Mednet Medical Ethics Connections
http://www.sermed.com/ethics.htm

Roslin Institute Online
http://www.ri.bbsrc.ac.uk

Wellcome Trust Online
http://www.wellcome.ac.uk

USEFUL ADDRESSES

AUSTRALIA

Centre for Human Bioethics
Monash University
Clayton, Victoria
Australia 3168

USA

Center for Bioethics
University of Pennsylvania
3401 Market Street 320
Philadelphia, PA 19104-3308

The Center for Bioethics and Human Dignity
2065 Half Day Road
Bannockburn, Il 60015

National Reference Center for Bioethics Literature
The Joseph and Rose Kennedy Institute of Ethics
Georgetown University
Washington DC 20057-1212

UK

Institute of Medical Ethics
Edinburgh Medical Group
Royal Infirmary of Edinburgh
Lauriston Place
Edinburgh EG3 9YW

Journal of Medical Ethics
Editor c/o Imperial College of Science
Technology and Medicine
14 Princes Gardens
London SW7 1NA

Ethics, Science and Information
British Medical Association
Tavistock Square
London WC1 9JR

INDEX